THE WOMAN
ON THE OTHER SIDE

Stephanie Conn

Doire Press

First published in 2016

Doire Press
Aille, Inverin
Co. Galway
www.doirepress.com

Layout & cover design: Lisa Frank
Cover image: Johnny Conn
Author photo: Johnny Conn

Printed by Clódóirí CL
Casla, Co. na Gaillimhe

ISBN 978-1-907682-42-1

A Captive Spirit by Marina Tsvetaeva, translated by J. Marin King (Virago, 1983), is reproduced with kind permission.

We gratefully acknowledge the assistance of The Arts Council of Northern Ireland.

LOTTERY FUNDED

CONTENTS

In memory of my mother
June Clegg
1950-1996

Wie is de Vrouw on de Overkant?

Who is the woman on the other side?
It was the only phrase that stuck
in months of pre-trip conversation class.

As I struggled with the syntax,
it became clear you were a natural,
spending hours in the lab perfecting your grasp.

You couldn't wait to track down a local
to ask how to say I love you? *Ik hou van you,*
you said, content with your acquisition.

You led me in the appropriate response,
encouraged me to practise daily. *Ik hou ook van you*
— all it took to keep you happy.

The towns we visited belonged to you,
their guttural place names all tongue and throat:
Groningen, Maastricht, Utrecht.

You strode through their stone streets
listing the features of gothic churches,
as I fumbled with a bi-lingual map.

Maria Annastraatje, Leeuwarden

The street is narrow, cobbled.
Tall houses rise on either side.
Only a thin rectangle of sky remains.

The door opens onto a steep stairway.
A rusting bike stands pressed against the wall.
Inside, Vermeer's viewpoint draws the eye.

Across the street, the only sign of life is flowers:
six single-stemmed gerbera daisies
stuck to the glass in plastic test-tubes.

Here, empty wine bottles sit on low white sills
dripping coloured wax from their plugged tops
and postcards of Klimt's paintings litter the floor.

Our bedroom has two doors. One leads to rooftops
and a metre square of shade. It's where I go to focus
on slate tiles tilting towards the sky.

Going Dutch

Strange now to think of single cells
splitting in that airy room
at the top of the stairs.

How later, words dripped away
in a single day and we laboured
to pronounce place names on a map of home.

We split the photos, the phantom booties,
one blue, one pink —
and never spoke of things again.

Dutch Bridges

There is a grey payphone attached to the wall.
When it rings I sometimes forget
and think it might be you.

I would tell you of the simple things —
how I leave the house too full of students
and walk the city's streets.

How the street stretches across the canal to the market stalls,
how the vendors call and hold up fruit or turn
to the child crying on the bridge. How I buy flowers.

How I pass the old clock and the chocolate shop,
where the windows will soon be stocked
with yellow bonnets and chicks.

How they serve tea in tall glasses without milk,
how in spring they'll set out wicker chairs
for people to sip their drinks and smoke cigarettes.

How back inside I'll cut the tulips' stems
and place them gently in the vase I bought last week —
blue delft, like the plate you inscribed with my birth date.

Delta

The dilapidated hut at the sand's edge
is a trick of the light, and shadows lift
to reveal a delicate arrangement of driftwood,
crate and rope; the uprooted debris of the sea.

Sunlight settles on a sodden sponge.

Here on a flat shelf of beach
disparities are ironed out;
faded plastic strips, origin unknown,
dull the glare of emerald glass.

Curious shallows slip to the shore.

Inland, the polder's stillness is not disturbed
by the pylons' hum or the clouds' insistent shift.
She is remembering the sea, its possibilities,
drained by the regulated tidiness of men.

The Ds Have It

The dictionary does not deliver
the definition I desire

but I discover

that delta rhythm is typical of sleep
that trees have deltoid leaves

that one should dig —
to delve is so archaic

and deltiology is best left
to holidaymakers.

Wadlopen

Not quite walking on water,
less of a miracle perhaps,
though equally unfamiliar
to wade the mudflats,
dark clay sucking at our boots.

Our young guide led us across
the seabed towards the islands,
took our guilders, asked us please
to heed the warnings; how quickly
water can rise on all sides,

how a fog can lead tourists,
like us, off course. How tide-tables
cannot protect against the shifts
in ebb and flow between the shallows
and the archipelago's belt.

Fierljeppen

With hindsight, he would not have tried
an alien custom such as this.
For one, he didn't have the height,
and truth be told, he leaped before he looked.

Farming wasn't in his blood,
there was no undiscovered ancestor
who might have vaulted plot to plot
over water-channels draining land.

He stood out in his unscuffed boots
that lugged his ankles, forcing slip.
His jump was sluggish, his climb weak
and the safety disk started to sink.

The local moved with forward sprint,
shimmied quickly up the pole,
propelled himself, distinguished jolt,
across the cold and muddy moat

to land gracefully on the sand,
then turned to watch the tourist type
teeter on a ten metre pole,
grasping madly at the light.

The Ice Race

We followed the canal path in the dark —
my gloved hand held by your bare palm
and I searched for words that might attend
to the task at hand but got distracted,
as our breath formed tiny spirits in the freezing air
and laughter in the distance cracked the silence.

We turned and saw at once a city alive at midnight.
The electric chatter of a thousand voices
lit up Main Street and we stood staring, mute.
It was the Nacht van Leeuwaarden, they said,
the night before the race, and as the temperatures
dropped the Friesian people danced and sang.

The skaters waited, contemplated eleven cities —
200 kilometres of frozen river between mud banks,
cards stamped at each historic point, each secret location
and all before the clock struck twelve. We learned that ice
must support all that it holds — 15 centimetres deep
throughout before a single blade can slice the surface.

Grandpa Paping

His grandchildren smirk when he talks of his win,
cannot imagine this shuffling man with the biscuit tin

speeding across the ice; still they listen to how he pressed
newspaper against his skin before he dressed —

a bid to stay warm in the freezing Hell of '63 —
ten hours, fifty-nine boys and the next man far behind me.

Head down into the eastern wind and the sub-zero
temperatures, to cross the line a national hero,

winner of the one percent who carried on regardless
for a free ice-rink pass and a silver cigarette case.

Beacon

All that remains of the gothic church
is an unfinished tower — its conspicuous tilt.

Despite the widened foundations, the added support,
the clock-tower sags under the weight

of the staircase; one hundred and twenty-seven
sandstone steps built against the north buttress.

We climbed the crooked staircase for the view;
the city stretched to the horizon, criss-crossed

by canals like bands of black silk
and a steeple piercing the New Year sky.

I knew then we would never visit Pisa.

Reflections

(Johannes Vermeer, *Girl Reading a Letter at an Open Window*)

I knew I would need air
and pulled the curtain back
to let it through into this cell
they like to call a room.

I knew that opening the window
wide at noon would stop me calling out
and the blue frame would steady
any bout of dizziness that might present

itself as unexpectedly as the letter.
Better to be prepared with two feet
firmly on the floor, and the door locked
tight, before you take a second look.

Vermeer's Nether Land

He painted the land that lies below —
led us through small windows, into narrow interiors,
half-lit rooms draped with silk and shadow
so we could peer at the mapped backdrops.

He mixed grains of sand into thick colour,
to make glass glitter and frame four meanings of horizon,
to draw the eye deeper and fuller,
to settle on the stillness of another's face.

He steeped the walls in illusions of white
that glowed blue, and shifted through ochre, amber, gold,
creating whispers of fluid light,
leaving us spellbound by silence.

Painting Light
(Johannes Vermeer, *Woman Holding a Balance*)

She removes her pearls

        sets them on the counter

with her golden chains

        to cool and collect dust

and moves instead to hold

        a balance between finger and thumb.

As a shaft of muted light

        settles on her ample belly

she grips the solid wood

        steadies herself with her free hand

avoids the mirrored glass

        and waits for the pans to still.

Mounds of blue silk cloth

        skirt coins in graduated stacks

and shifting skies cast

        shadows in the corner but illuminate

the scales — holding nothing

        but drops of precious light.

View from a Rocking Chair
(Edward Hopper, *Room in Brooklyn*, 1932)

She sets the chair far enough back
to make the street disappear
so the windows frame rooftops.

The horizon is flat but for red-brick chimneys
blunt against the blue expanse of cloudless sky.
She looks down nonetheless.

Fine black hair slips to skim her face,
exposes the curve of her neck,
naked flesh above the high buttoned dress.

In a slant of afternoon light,
five wooden slats keep her back straight,
the chair kept steady by her well-placed feet.

The table is out of reach. Its carved wood
covered by a plain blue cloth,
a porcelain vase placed carefully on top.

She loves its symmetry; a logical choice
for white roses that blush in the sun
and bend slightly towards the altered light.

The Village
(Marc Chagall, *I and the Village*, 1911)

Look me in the eye that I might see the memory
that makes your jaw grow tense and your cheeks flush
red as fallen apples scattered beside the village wall.

Tell me of the green fields mapped in your mind
and the winding paths that always lead you back,
how your father held a scythe in his dark hands,

taught you to hold the blade close to the ground,
move clockwise from the meadow's edge, while a man
milked the goat under a blue sky, how you once held

ripened figs in your hands and the branches glowed
in the changing light, that you circled back to her street,
how the world shrank and turned full tilt to the sound

of her violin, sent you spinning, like the coloured lights
draped on lemon trees in the village square, and reaching
for the silver cross pressed against your throat.

The Duel
(Alexander Naumov, *Pushkin's Duel*, 1884)

I still recall the picture —
black sapling branches against snow
and the wounded Pushkin held upright.
The pistol shot to his stomach sends me reeling
back to the undersea under-piano world —
the palms, the pots of philodendrons, their green light;
mother's foot on the gold pedal, her music pouring down,
the white keys always happy, the black reliably sad.
I see myself sneaking out, once she has left the room,
to blow on the most sacred surface in the house,
hurrying to press my face onto the sheer black lake,
printing puffed lips on my own receding breath
knowing the piano will take away my mouth.

The Metronome

In my life there are several firmly fixed joys: not to go to the Gymnasium, not to wake up in Moscow of 1919 and not to hear a metronome.

— Marina Tsvetaeva

Tick-tock
I am four —
I want to live in a cuckoo clock
emerge on the hour from the wooden door
to call my call.

Tick-tock
I am six —
straight-backed on a black stool as a steel stick
oscillates, its methodical click
measuring my days.

Tick-tock
I am eight —
I want to live in a bright street-light
peer at the path or up to the sky and wait
to speak to the stars.

Tick-tock
I am ten —
lead-legged on the parquet floor as mother
sneers at the words that flowed from my pen
and rips the book.

Tick-tock
I am twelve —
I want to live in Valeria's room
touch powders, pills, scent bottles on shelves
lock myself in.

Tick-tock
I am grown —
know now that love is sharply felt in parting
for she played her last note, left me alone
free at fourteen.

Tick-tock
I am old —
the clock sends shivers through my clicking spine
the power of the *lifeless over the living* told
in the steady beat.

Is that the Sea?

That's not the sea at all, not at all like the sea.

— Marina Tsvetaeva

They named me Marina for the Black Sea,
said my dark hair rose and fell like the waves
I'd never seen. How your words convinced me,
Pushkin. Your lines tell it well. Image weaves
image of your vast unharnessed ocean,
your talk of breakers' lips, the lure of sway,
your azure sea swells in endless motion.
This pale grey monster that lives in the bay
instantly crushes a child's devotion.
These drifting ridges chill. I walk away
to stroll upright on my mountains, listen
to birdsong rise without the commotion
of the slippery sea's resounding display.
The appeal of rock will never lessen.

Her Diaries

All notes have plummeted from the page,
All revelations from the mouth…

— Marina Tsvetaeva

It is June
but the curtains are pulled
and the candles lit.

In an empty room
a fourteen year old girl
pores over her mother's diaries.

The piano keys
are still. Words on the page
dictate a new melody.

There will be
no more nodding birds
no more sparrows on their designated branches.

Even the swans
she etched on the stave can go
question marks replace crochets.

In the nine bound volumes
she discovers a woman she never knew
someone who had loved once.

There in that last book
after her mother's final word — *but* —
she finds a thick wad of stumps

and almost wishes her back to life.

The Portrait of His First Wife

They stand
face to face
his two wives —

no, not quite.
The young one, seventeen,
still has her feet on the ground.

She looks up
to the other, hung high
on the drawing-room wall.

The beauty gazes back,
smiles with her dark eyes,
her mouth as delicate as a bird's.

The girl walks
to a tall window, looks out
at the silver poplar leaning across the gate.

A growing daughter
quickens at her centre, drives her on
through the rooms of this wooden house.

And she waits
for the strong wail of a son
to drive out the song of all her nights —

the call of a nightingale
emerging softly from beneath
the locked door, to sooth a living boy.

Blinking in the Dark

If you have placed your hands, at their urging, on the new wet skull,
small as a cat's, and recoiled in surprise at the slippery touch
of matted hair, despite the months of waiting, of willing this moment
to arrive, then you too can go back to the start of it all;
to that moment in the dark, eyes shut and alert to every touch
when I caught my breath, and you took it and made it your own
and surged blindly on, splitting to become whole; of course,
we were totally unaware in the instant we set you ticking (busy talking)
but that night I dreamt of rain, or heard it on the window pane —
persistent drops that fell and found the swell of a lake or river and made
for the open sea; I thickened as shadows pulsed on screens and lines peaked
and fell long before the quickening that made you, finally, real —
you held on tight, where others had faltered, and were content to watch
a tiny hand open and close in that watery room until the walls shuddered
in their bid to expel and you emerged and cried out into the light —
our cord cut, they carried you off to count your fingers and toes,
the vertebrae of your still-curved spine, checking for tell-tale signs
that you might be less than perfect; they did not see the cord take form
or hear it hiss as it slithered upward, past my breast and I lay caught,
lead-legged and tied to machines, as it rose up, ready to swallow me whole.

I hear their laughter from another room

it strikes somewhere beneath my ribs,
its music is palpable enough
to season this sauce with its sweetness.
I squirt lemon into the pot
and feel the sting as the acid grips
the tiny cut on my hand.

I can imagine the scene — my husband
rising in stature under her gaze.
His wine untouched
he will drink from her eyes,
those wide innocent eyes.
Drunk on her approval
and her zest for life
he will become all that he was.

In the pot, the pasta boils.
The heat rises and the water
starts to hiss and spit.
The knife cuts through the crusty bread
as beads of sweat drip
down the panes of glass.

Should I march down the hall
or creep, to witness first hand
this tender unravelling
this ancient dance of devotion?
Or stand barefoot in the kitchen
stirring pasta, lest it stick,
and turn the radio up
as some tribal chant rises in my throat?

I follow the sound. He is vibrant.
I recall that look on his face,
those creases as familiar to me
as the cracks on our bedroom ceiling.
They are at their beginning.
I see that he is her world
and though tears threaten and sting,
I cannot tear myself away.

And to think I introduced them.
Delivered her into his waiting hands,
bloodied, wrinkled, screaming, new.
I, still dazed by the lights
and by being
separate.

Bangor

Back then there was a stretch of beach
for sunny days at the bottom of Main Street,
years before the new marina was complete
when the tide was still within reach.

There was a high wall, steep grey steps
that led to sand, just enough to please a child
who gathered water in a bucket and smiled
at bathers as her granny slept

open-mouthed on a green deck chair.
She looked out at the huge ships heading for dock
triangles of deep blue on Belfast Lough
pulled taut by the late April air.

The unseen glass sliced through her skin
and she screamed at the sight of so much red blood
seeping into the sand and rushed to flood
the gaping wound. The taste of tin

in her mouth made her drop and gag
salt stinging her eyes as she knelt by the shore
then back on her feet, she hobbled, stiff and sore,
to throw away the bloody rag.

Though the spot where she bled is gone
buried beneath concrete, black seats, dwarf trees
and iron railings hold her back from the seas,
the faint track of a scar lives on.

What We Pass On

I have taken to throwing them into the sea.

I always go alone, drive the car
to the rough ground behind the dunes.
Sometimes passers-by raise their brows
wonder if there is a law against it.

Usually I wait for darkness.

In my hands I hold nothing but keys.
A bitter wind blows salt in my eyes.
Even in winter it seems right to go
barefoot to where the water's lapping.

I do it slowly

let them go one by one, making sure to unhinge
the most stubborn stains and bruises
that still reside in the frontal lobe
searching out receptive transmitters

the view inside an empty church

the weight of your hand on my shoulder
the other tightening a grip on my waist
the blackness that fell with astonishing speed
even though my eyes were wide open.

The stark echo of a hundred lies

how you grew giant with rage, reduced us
to stick men, whittled away into the night.
The wedge you used was stone, cold
as your stare, grey as your gritted teeth.

I offload the deaths last —

the memory of your hands shaking
the buttery crumbs falling onto the bed
the smell of too many chrysanthemums
just as the petals dropped.

These things I give to the sea

break off their edges
and round their ragged remains
so my children can handle them safely
when they find them washed up on the beach.

The Last Photograph

A candle flickers beside a miniature Santa.
We are gathered round the table, ready
for the first course: lemon-drizzled prawns
smothered in sauce spill from red glass dishes
brought out for the occasion. But first,
a snap shot to remember you by.

Staged smiles plastered across faces.
Yours is the worst, like it has been thrust
through some cartoon-clad holiday board
that shouts, I'm having fun! despite the rain
and the quarrel in the car over where to park.
Nobody's fooled. Wait. My sister's smile is real —

she thinks your hair is growing back.
The flash creates a halo above the tight crop
of grey hair that once shone honey blonde.
The potatoes dry and thicken in my mouth.
Your plate is swimming in gravy as you shovel
spoonfuls of ham into your twitching mouth.

That morning I watched you work
but could not ask how best to cook the turkey, and later,
as the light slipped out of the garden and you raged
at the broken cupboard door, nearly raised the roof with a rant
I'd never heard the like of, I too had to pretend this was the worst
that could happen and focus on the bolt and the door hanging from its hinge.

That She May Always Have Roses

She watches from the window
as he hauls slabs of Scrabo stone
to the front of the house

stacks the irregular brick
smoothes the cement evenly
to secure the border edge

builds the rectangular frame
to contain all the colour
and fragrance of the flowers.

She leaves the door ajar and walks outside
pulls a sweater tight around her shoulders
despite the spring sunshine

hands him the pruning gloves
the rusty shears, and asks the names
of the red buds, the pink, the white.

He prepares the beds, plants each one
but has enough stone left over to build a path
from her rose garden to the red-brick wall.

Canadian Christmas

Dropping down to land I saw
the tops of trees like broccoli and shivered
at the sight of homes lined up like wooden sheds,
glad my case was filled with woollen socks
and sweaters, bundled up like loaves of bread.

On Christmas Day we circled the block
all brushed of snow, and stopped
to watch the heavy flakes ignore the fact
and layer every path and drive,
their timing unremitting and exact.

We took too many photographs
the shutter relentless until it stuck —
and it clicked in the white silence.
Later, round the table we passed the plates
and thought — you sat here once.

But that was years ago and in the heat
of summer. The basement proved cool enough
to spend an hour listening to the hum of a drying machine,
folding laundry, matching socks. It was the perfect place
to hide, knowing everything could be washed clean.

Cutting lemons

and thinking of nothing but the chop
I am suddenly back in my grandmother's flat
pinching delicate leaves between finger and thumb
rubbing gently to gather their lemon scent on my skin
careful not to rip the plant or drop the china saucer to the floor

and my fingertips grow stained with the thick red juice
from picking loganberries off the bush at the back
of my grandfather's house and my mouth smarts
with the tang of seeds on my tongue and I feel tiny
hairs tickle my throat as I swallow them whole

and I am lifting pineapple chunks to your lips
so you might suck the sweetness and remember
flavour and how you once walked on the cool sand
sipping a Piña colada under a tropical moon — a blade
slices my skin and my mouth is filled with the taste of tin.

Sulphur Mining

From another angle you might be taken in
by the turquoise hue of the crater lake
might meditate on fallen clouds or cooling mists
or stop to breathe, hidden from sight.

But look
as the light reveals the jagged rocks
that gag on noxious gases
and spew out vomit laced with blood.

Look closer —
these are not scuttling volcano-beetles
scavenging for food, but men
scaling the sides to feed their children and their wives.

Men with rags stuffed in their mouths
trying not to breathe as they crouch close to the edge
fingering the bruised incline, slipping
their scarred hands back into the fire to rip at brimstone.

Twice a day they haul their load
onto bulging shoulders to climb the rocky paths
as the steam seeps deeper down
into their lungs and teeth dissolve.

Look —
their eyes are bright as the acid lake
that strips the garish colours
from discarded tins and leaves them white.

Absolute Desert

It has been pouring for days and in a country such as this
it is hard to imagine the driest place on earth
but at Atacama's centre the loose lying sediment
proclaims a lack of that which might wash it all away —
millions of years without a single drop of rain.

Here nothing rots, the dead remain preserved forever dead
between the barren hills and freezing desert nights.
Yet further south, algae and lichen make the most
of marine fog and perennials, and woody scrub
suck on clouds entrapped by faulted mountains.

And though the arid plains are littered with abandoned
nitrate mining towns, the Peruvian song-sparrows sing
and lemons still grow on the shores of the salt marshes
while the villagers in Chungungo catch fog in mesh nets
so moisture can condense and trickle into copper troughs.

Mercury

1.

To be this close to the sun and still exist, orbiting
in your own eccentric way, albeit in extremes.
And us peering through lenses for your secrets
while you halt, reverse, resume at speed.
What message do you bring from the gods?
Fry or freeze. What can you teach? What can you unleash
that won't be burnt to dust and blasted from the surface
by some solar wind? Your core — all depth, all density,
your outer shell, just that.

2.

Mercury, safely encased — the thermometer speaks —
her words are fluid and warn of water turning into ice
or the risk of solids melting in the rising heat,
guarding carefully against the element of chance;
of being caught unawares on some freezing peak
wearing open-toed shoes, or languishing on desert sands
where nothing can live but poisonous, shrivelled, spiky things —
and the long-eared rabbits, the squirrels and toads, the birds
and the willow, poppies, marigolds — vital, in the midday sun.

Eclipse

They said it would happen,
warned not to observe the sun
directly. I had been indoors

discussing flowers with a stranger,
the pros and cons of delphiniums
pale blue hydrangeas, the availability

of snowdrops and forget-me-nots in winter,
the daintiness of stephanotis, the cost.
I flicked through plastic-covered pictures

then left, arms brimming with pages
torn from magazines, aware of the choice,
stuck on the one that mattered.

I was stunned when the light
shunned the morning, and although I knew
it was only the moon passing

tears came quickly and I stood
stock-still in the shadow, counting
the seconds at the pavement's edge.

Lepus

Their collective noun is *drove*
though they mostly live alone
content with a solitary life

or become one of a pair
growing brave in the spring;
chests puffed out as if

fluid has filled the cavities
and dropsy has caused a long-forgotten
frenzy, that gives rise

to a meadow dash in daylight
or a moonlit boxing match
below the moon hare's dark patches —

that ancient celestial ancestor —
as a distant cousin is driven south
by the hunter and his dogs.

Making Up the Numbers

Each year a single star is born
to reignite the passion of those who find it
name it, point it out, observe it closely
and give pleasure to those astronomers grown tired
of mapping the same familiar patch of illuminated black.

The rest of us make up the numbers
present enough sparkling dots in the sky
to create a perfect pattern of a chariot or throne
though the odd one wanders off course, rising
shattering the equilibrium, going giant with rage.

The Display

We drew them in daylight,
plotted stars on black paper
to the sound of pencils being sharpened
and boys whispering by the bin.

We connected the dots in white chalk
to see, more clearly, the shapes they made,
watched the outline become a rainbow
as layer after layer left behind
tiny mounds of coloured dust.

Yesterday we talked of stories in the sky,
learned how to spell con-stell-ation,
how a winged horse and a hunter's dog
hide above our heads until we sleep.

I read in a book that chalk is formed
from the skeletons of sea creatures
how things we've never seen can become
something else entirely in our hands.
Today I mapped a cello in the sky.

Halley's Comet

He said he would only see it once
then traced an ellipse in the sand
but we, being young, might chance

to see it twice in our lifetime.
The night he looked up
the cloud was thick, the climb

concealed. The comet nears the sun,
warms, begins to sublimate,
the volatile compounds transform.

Gas radiates around the nucleus
dust particles scatter ice
and solar light goes nebulous.

I dream her into the sky —
a brilliant apparition —
and see close-up the ink-dyed

surface, the varied topography
of mountains and craters,
commit her ridges to memory.

Space pulls her ions out into a tail
as she moves to her perihelion
beyond the moon; the chaotic trail

of a retrograde orbit almost done.
The sum of her travels mapped, predictions
made, for late July, twenty sixty-one.

August Moons
after Neil Armstrong

This month it seems that one is not enough
and night offers up her full glow for a second time
as though nature herself wished to honour you.

Quietly the calendar waits for the moon to catch up.
Silent days drawn to the pull of a distant light,
her steady orbit. The lunacy of man steps out

from the cycle of hours, cuts through space at speed
to soar above a ball of blue and white and walk on silver
dust to speak measured words from his helmeted mouth.

Abacus

June. Again.
There have been too many
birthdays and deathdays.

Two black stars
marked on the calendar
five squares apart.

Once the date
flashed red beside a clock
in the bank —

sent the coins
crashing to the marble
floor; scattered orbs

of bronze and gold —
an empty money bag
gripped in my hand.

Signs and Superstitions

When you broke the wings off the angel
I tried not to mind, for you were only a child,
and told myself it was not a sign but lit a candle
nonetheless, watched the white wax drip on a mild
August night and looked for patterns in the sky,
pulsing points of light through a tilted window.
I spotted the Plough and the Bear, and wondered why
we search for comfort in the stars, when down below
the earth offers up her well-trodden lanes and roads
and we know those who have seen it all before
can talk us through the path they took at the crossroads
or tell us how they made their choice and walked out the door.
For days I gathered feathers wherever they could be found,
no doubt from quilts or pillows or from a passing bird.
I looked both ways at crossings, waited for the sound
of crashing glass, avoided cats and ladders, absurd
I know, a pagan prayer of sorts, I jumped the cracks,
crossed my fingers and scattered the jacks.

Inca Ice Maiden

The light will reveal
at the touch of a switch
the body of a sleeping child
behind the glass, like an open
hand scooped, ready to receive.

Her head is bowed and lice remain
in the tight braids that fall about her
face and cover her eyes. Visitors come
to peer at the fine hairs visible on her arms,
the hands in her lap, the grey shawl adorned

with metal and bone; those fine threads pulled
round her slim neck five centuries before, ready
to follow the mountain path up towards the gods
and the thinning air. All her life she'd been prepared
for this — handpicked — just like the priests, statues, gold,

the coca leaf and chica for the child, the north facing tomb.
Did you speak from beyond the icy grave as they gave thanks
or choke on your frozen tongue when they named you goddess?
Plucked from the pit, did you feel the lurch? Taken from the heavens
and thawed, your blood poured out like that of a living child, crimson and pure.

Driven

Mastering love in adolescence —
better to have stayed inside reading lies
than trying to shovel the relentless swell of snow.
The spade struck the bottle with a crack —
tomorrow's milk seeping out onto the frozen drift.
Shattered underfoot, broken glass shone in the moonlight.
Yes, better to have stayed inside, than greet those prodding fingers
pilfering her youth. *Delectable,* he shuddered, as though
appraising a personal masterpiece. He didn't care
to read between the lines, didn't care for
the bold, plain print, or for the girl
playing grown up.

Cherry Blossom

This year the blush has been purged
from the blossoms, leaving them white
and at the mercy of the wind.

Above, the bare blue sky grows bruised,
a narrow sheet of light escapes, illuminates
black branches holding nothing but air.

Contusion

Strange to note the iridescent patch
of pearly white on tanned skin
that once plumped pink.

This skin knows too much
so begins to forget
how to heal as quickly as it did.

Pinprick Work

Till I poor convict greets my liberty.

For seven months she rubbed the penny smooth
and learned to read and write, and saw his name
engraved upon the coin and wrote her own beside an X.

Below the deck she watched them perforate
their skin and dab the wound with ink or soot
to make the *without hope* turn black.

Before they docked she raised her cotton sleeve,
carefully scooped the sediment from the lamp,
made circles with her fingertips. *I love to the heart.*

Enjoy Your Stay
Port Arthur, 1870

Welcome. You have progressed
from the penitentiary
to the separate jail.

Here, we keep the peace —
note the felt slippers covering our boots,
the sea-grass laid out on the concrete floor.

To the right is your cell —
feel free to spend your twenty-three
isolated hours behind this door.

Walking will be done alone —
your remaining time in the high-walled yard.
We will be out of sight moving like ghosts.

Absconders Beware

Jones laid out a strip of cockle shells
across the road to show his plan:
a line of lamps and nine
ferocious dogs
to bare their
grin at any
soul who
dared to
cross the
narrow
stretch
of land
some
call a
neck.
Even
if the
sentries
slept at
their posts
the slightest
noise from the
bush would have
the mutts' ears twitching
and their throats growling, teeth
ready to puncture skin, to convince
the bravest of men with their own blood.

Salvage
Boxing Day, 1952

They rescued the paintings,
left the ship behind
lodged on a sandbank
beyond Wineglass Bay,

brought them by road to Hobart
where students gathered at the dock,
grins spread across each young face
as they lugged them up the back stairs

in their bare hands — Duffy, Gromaire, Rouault,
Picasso, Picabia, L'Hove —
and hung them on a hessian frame
taking care not to step on Matisse's sky

or crumple his lapping blue, the starfish, the shells.
The Beautiful Summer shone —
the coloured weft — green, yellow, red —
weaving corn to brick and smoke to tree,

rich tapestries that would shift as they slept
colouring their own canvas strokes, memories
that would journey on under the Southern Cross
and out into the open sea.

Travelling the Distance
State Library of New South Wales

Looking up, I catch the change as fibre optics flick
from blue to white and hear the hush of turning pages.
Here, the stars' position in the sky is fixed — clear Perspex,
stainless steel and cobalt glass cement a constellation.

Underneath, heels click around a mosaic marble map;
Wombeyan russet slabs, 20 millimetres thick, depicting
Tasman's journey to the South. Above the illustrated waves
the cursive script is dark — *Campagnis Niev Nederland.*

Solstice Art

1.

Tourists swarm the ice-cream cart
or shuffle to the Palm House.
The glass sweats beside a sun
set down on canvas and they
point to the highest frame,
watching the paint swirl around
dots splattered in a southern sky.

2.

The sun rises in the North.
A strip of light stretches
along a megalithic tomb,
illuminates a cruciform chamber,
its chiselled curves of rock
on rock. The spirits of the dead
ignite, at last, and rise like dust.

Wurrungwuri

To see a stationary wave of sandstone blocks
cascade towards the Harbour Bridge

seems less strange than a black cross woven into rock
on a monolith built from pebbles of threaded quartz.

They say, at night, you can hear the wings of bats flap
as they leave their box, hidden inside the stagnant sea

and that the cross glows violently in the moonlight
when they settle in the roped-off Wollemi Pine.

Penguin Watching on Redbill Beach

Out of place in this heat
this sweltering air, hairdryer-hot
we wait for the temperature drop of twilight.

For years I have taught
six year olds to stick cut-out penguins
on A3 sheets of ice and snow.

Now we wait on the east coast
in cut-off jeans, to catch a glimpse
of their tiny frames, one ruler tall.

There are others here
Fuji Finepix slung around their necks
like magic pendants

catching the moonlight
sending blasts of light crashing
onto the bare rocks.

We wait. Watch them leave
cursing at the sea, let the breeze shake
free of their disappointed voices.

The penguins have found
another way. Two tap their way out
of the waves, try the sandy gap

between stone. They hop onto
a low lying rock and flat-foot it
to the trees. The rest follow

a single line of shuffling feet
like small children filing from a classroom
clutching text books under their arms.

Fair Trade

after Lyn Reeves' 'Maireener Shells'

Forgive me. It is less my story to tell than yours, and yet
having come to hear it spoken from your lips, I know
it can travel great distances. I long to tell my children

how the Palawa women sat by the kerosene lamps stringing
shells on the sinew of kangaroo tail, kept wet for the stretch,
the natural grease letting them slip easily into place.

How they left the miniature cones swept up on the beach
alone, knowing they'd be brittle. Waded out, instead,
in the low spring tides until they were waist deep in water,

pulled the living shells from the seaweed fronds, watched
the drops of iridescent green and violet gleam in their dripping
hands. Back on sand, they smoked their haul and rubbed them

gently in the long grass to reveal the lustre of their pearly base.
The young girls of the tribe soaked up every move the elders made
in moonlight, how they bore holes with the eye-tooth of a wallaby

putting just enough pressure on the point, never shattering the shell.
They carried their loot home to the lull of tales retold and the delicate
click of their catch against thighs. They counted their blessings

into intricate patterns, watched them fall in long shining loops
feeling a familiar ache in their fingers. Soon they would trace red
ochre onto their skin in spirals, whispering thanks to the sea.

Their story isn't mine to tell and yet I know it by heart. My
daughters carry it with them, and when they gather periwinkles
at low tide on this island beach, they open their hands to the waves.

Midnight Storm

There was no warning
unless you count the sight of a wallaby
bouncing between pavements
before sloping up the hill.

Our shack still stood on its stilts
at the top of the steep incline
its back pressed against
the tinder-dry earth.

You climbed the wooden steps
the baby swaddled in a sling
her warm body slung across
your sweating skin and leaking breasts.

The lightning ripped open the sky
the rumble drowned out the cry of our charge
you held your breath knowing there was nothing
between us and the clouds. I photographed the strike.

Flashback

She dreams of lightning over Bicheno Bay —
a wide-angle shot of ocean, inky black and waiting,
shivering beyond the arc of rock and sand.

A fluorescent strike finds a shell below the surface.
Close-up and just a hint of pearlescent lining,
the magnified view of nacre, concentric layer

upon layer, the accelerated motion forming a bead.
Cross-cut to the perfect drop resting in the small dip
of tanned skin beneath her throat. She is wearing white.

A wide-shouldered man in a dark suit stands in soft-focus.
Freeze-frame. She is choking, waking, staring at a stranger
on a sea-blue pillow, open-mouthed, centimetres from her face.

The Ring

She did not know rejection
could cause such lustre
could be a luminescent gem
composed entirely of nacre.

She watched him take it from the box
and name it — *keshi* pearl.
He had not known a mollusc
could spit out its core, could curl

layers of its glinting moisture
around a fleck of shell or scale
could form a shimmering thumbprint
on a prayer. She could feel

his eyes on hers, and then he spoke
to fill the silence, explained its meaning
— *poppy seed* — in Japanese. She liked
that but couldn't see it happening

could see the shape but not the colour.
It was set in white gold, not stone — *say
something!* Perhaps another
bead would look less ghostly grey.

Poppy Crop

The word jumps on the tongue
smacks of dry pods
and black seeds
blood.

Here, they are the colour of tears
light blue handkerchiefs
blinking in December
sun.

I'm told their oil kills pain.
To keep clear of the fields
and the border
fence.

Perhaps I should plant a time-
capsule, paint what I see:
the small mountain
bluffs

the single eucalypt tree
a river; include a letter —
u or y — bury it.
Leave.

When You Leave

When you leave I relax into steady breaths,
slip upstairs into the back room, leaving
the dishwasher unstacked, the beds unmade.
I fail to phone the doctor for results
or collect the mail strewn in the hall.
I do not pair the mismatched socks.
Instead I close the bedroom door,
step over the accumulated stuff
that remains, year in, year out:
cardboard boxes of Christmas stars,
monitors, nightlights, stair-gates,
cases filled with baby clothes.

I find a dusty shoebox —
the small one labelled *me*
and rifle through its contents;
pages from a diary ripped out in a fit,
a mixed tape from '88, square snaps
from back in the day of waiting
and proofs. They span so many years.
You are not in a single shot.
In each picture there is a missing part,
some trick of the light, a shadow here or there,
a smudged thumb, a missing hand or foot
and in this final one — the heart.

Sleep

is at its most alluring just
as the alarm clock sends its shrill
command into the dark and the arrows
released in dreams are sent

showering into sleepy wake, to pierce
the skin with their tut, tut, tutting
to inflict, again and again, their disapproving
faces, and though the air seems to quiver

like heat rising in rings above dry earth
(where a gaggle of old hens peck in the dirt)
their raised eyebrows and tight lips
seem cast in solid ice. But it is your lips

I can feel on mine and I bite down on flesh
just to draw blood. Bedroom walls
find their rightful lines and settle into place
and the moment is lost in the thud of tiny feet

missing out stairs, the clatter of spoons,
the chatter, the spilled sugar, the quarrel
over a pink plate. And all day long
I try to get back, to follow that silvery

thread round corners, upstairs
and at last I find it, cut
and hanging in the
still air.

Lavender Fields

We hide between the land's contours until they leave,
resist the temptation to sleep on the still-warm ground
intoxicated by the shrub's scent clinging to our skin.

All this grew from a small bag of aromatic seeds
taken from high in the French Alps and planted
here, at just the right altitude, in the red soil.

Precious cargo carried from their London perfumery
to Van Diemen's Land, along the lanes past Lilydale
to Nabowla, to settle on this vista fit for the strain.

We wait to see the last sun setting, backs pressed
against the massive oak, speak only in whispers.
No-one in the world hears. No-one knows we are here.

Without local varieties to cross-pollinate or corrupt
their perfect crop, they stayed, worked the empty fields,
placed the fragrant drops into the earth in curves.

The lilac moon keeps us alert, that and our finger tips.
When the solstice sun rises over the mountain we are
feasting on lavender honey, our eyes glowing amber.

Vinification

after Louise Oxley's 'Olive'

Wine, vino, vin: their sounds move through a kiss from subtle lips
to a tongue-tap behind the teeth and a curled 'o' before leaving you
open-mouthed as if a half-formed thought still hangs in the air.

Now, having fed for twenty years off the grapevine,
I get to look you in the eye over a glass of Pinot Noir
and try to recall if your lips always had this stain.

You explain fermentation in glorious detail; chemical
breakdown never sounded so sweet. I distil your words
and the long steady silences that surround them.

They say wine talks; perhaps after all this time we speak
different languages, so press our palms together, as if in prayer,
then lace our fingers. Tomorrow we will head for the hills.

We meander the valley, read tourist signs: the aboriginal name
for this place is *Kooparoona Niara*. We try it on our tongues.
In the foothills of the Tiers we happen upon a cellar door.

Inside others sit in clusters trying to decipher the top notes
and the delicate variations in the swirl of cool liquid.
We step outside and find an empty table in the sun.

In the fields the workers stay focused on their tasks — pluck
grapes from the woody vines and hand-press them to release
what they've been holding all season. Our warm mouths meet.

Further up, the mountains grow ragged and the land is littered
with burnt tree stumps, each one blackened by forest fire.
We have reached the Plateau marked clearly on the map.

We spread a picnic rug to share cucumber and fennel salad, peaches, honey-soaked walnut cake. With the sun on my neck, a fully-formed thought strikes — Dionysus was twice-born.

Annaghmakerrig

I am fifty metres from the lake,
yet it is dry here and raining there —
the burst shifts to drench the house
and I am quenched for thirty seconds
or less, until the sudden thud of bird
on glass. The heart stops, races
and in an instant the sky is blue and shining,
the stones already gathering dust.

Three Seconds

Anything could happen
in the time it takes
a snail to see the light.

Milking Snails

The snails slip across the isolated coral,
protected by the body whorl of their golden shells.
Spikes line the years beyond the siphonal canal.

The Phoenicians knew their secret, would poke
and prod the prize from their glands,
strip the predatory mollusc of its milky mucus

and wait to see the colourless liquid turn
purple when exposed to air. The dye did not fade
but grew permanent and more intense with weathering.

Tessellation

All it took
was a light dusting of snow
to transform the concrete slabs
in the yard into the tops of Roman heads,
crowned with laurel leaves.

The senate meet
to discuss the progress made,
the pipes channelling waste out of the city,
the water, siphoned in from some distant valley
lounging, as if in steaming baths, between the hills.

I follow their roads
out into the countryside; green cassias
gather by the stream where the air is thick
with saffron and the keeper, busy with his bees,
sprinkles dust to count the kings.

Cow-dung smeared on fennel-stems
congeals in the blistering sun, and honey
starts to bubble in the glutted combs.
Is that Virgil standing by the hives,
his breath heavy with the scent of thyme?

The snow is already melting and tomorrow
I will kneel on the cold stone and prepare
to plant pollen-rich flowers
in readiness, along
the border wall.

ACKNOWLEDGEMENTS

Acknowledgements are due to the following publications in which versions of these poems first appeared: *Abridged, Banshee, Burning Bush 2, Community Arts Partnership Anthologies: Making Memories, The Poet's Place & Still, Crannóg, Decanto, Derry Post, Five, FourXFour, Lighthouse, Open Ear, Panning for Poems, Paper Girl, Pickled Body, Poetry Bus, Shift, Skylight 47, Southword, Stony Thursday Book, Turbulence, Ulster Tatler, Wordlegs* and *Yellow Nib*.

'Lavender Fields' won the inaugural Seamus Heaney Award for New Writing in 2015, hosted by Community Arts Partnership. 'When You Leave' was shortlisted for the Seamus Heaney Award. 'Tessellation' was shortlisted in the Red Line Poetry Competition. 'The Village' was shortlisted in the Anam Cara Poetry Competition. Selections of poems were shortlisted for the Patrick Kavanagh Poetry Award and highly commended in the Doire Press Poetry Chapbook Competition, Fool for Poetry Chapbook Competition and Mslexia Poetry Pamphlet Competiton.

I am grateful to Newtownabbey Borough Council for a Tyrone Guthrie Bursary. A number of these poems were written or completed at the centre in Annaghmakerrig.

Thanks are due to the Arts Council of Northern Ireland and the National Lottery for a Support for Individual Artists Award in 2013 and a Career Enhancement Award in 2014.

Thanks are also due to Ciaran Carson, Moyra Donaldson, Sinéad Morrissey, Medbh McGuckian and Damian Smyth for their direction and encouragement; to Emma Must for her invaluable feedback; to Johnny Conn for proofreading with such care and for his support in so many other ways; to Ards Writers for helping pave the way; to my poetry gig buddies Kathy Finlay and Jillian McPeake; and finally to John Walsh and Lisa Frank at Doire Press for making this book a reality.

The Tasmania poems are dedicated to Helen Carlisle. Thanks are due to Louise Oxley and Lyn Reeves who were happy for me to write and include response pieces to their poems *Olive* and *Maireener Shells*.

STEPHANIE CONN was born in County Down in 1976 and now lives in County Antrim with her husband and two daughters. A graduate of Stranmillis University College, she worked as a primary school teacher and developed and taught the literacy programme Passport to Poetry. In 2013 Stephanie graduated from the Creative Writing M.A. Programme at the Seamus Heaney Centre, Queens University, Belfast.

In 2012 Stephanie was shortlisted for the Patrick Kavanagh Award and Anam Cara Competition and highly commended in the Doire Press Poetry Chapbook and Mslexia Poetry Pamphlet competitions. The following year she was shortlisted in the Red Line Poetry Competition and her work was selected for the Poetry Ireland Introductions Series. In 2014 she was highly commended in the Fool for Poetry Chapbook competition and won the Translink Haiku Competition. In 2015 she came third in the Dromineer Poetry Competition, was Highly Commended in the Gregory O'Donoghue Competition and was awarded the Funeral Services NI Poetry Prize, the Yeovil Poetry Prize and the inaugural Seamus Heaney Award for New Writing. She is currently working on her second collection.